IT'S TIME TO LEARN ABOUT ARCTIC FOX

It's Time to Learn about Arctic Fox

Walter the Educator

Silent King Books
A WhichHead Entertainment Imprint

Copyright © 2025 by Walter the Educator

All rights reserved. No part of this book may be reproduced in any manner whatsoever without written per- mission except in the case of brief quotations embodied in critical articles and reviews.

First Printing, 2024

Disclaimer

This book is a literary work; the story is not about specific persons, locations, situations, and/or circumstances unless mentioned in a historical context. Any resemblance to real persons, locations, situations, and/or circumstances is coincidental. This book is for entertainment and informational purposes only. The author and publisher offer this information without warranties expressed or implied. No matter the grounds, neither the author nor the publisher will be accountable for any losses, injuries, or other damages caused by the reader's use of this book. The use of this book acknowledges an understanding and acceptance of this disclaimer.

It's Time to Learn about Arctic Fox is a collectible early learning book by Walter the Educator suitable for all ages belonging to Walter the Educator's Time to Eat Book Series. Collect more books at WaltertheEducator.com

USE THE EXTRA SPACE TO TAKE NOTES AND DOCUMENT YOUR MEMORIES

ARCTIC FOX

Way up north, where it's cold and white,

It's Time to Learn about
Arctic Fox

Lives a fox so small and bright.

With fur so thick and paws so light,

It walks through snow both day and night.

The Arctic fox is built for chill,

Its fluffy coat is warm and still.

It changes color through the year,

In winter white, in summer clear!

Its tiny ears and furry feet,

Help it stay so warm and neat.

It curls up tight when winds do blow,

And hides beneath the ice and snow.

With a nose so sharp and ears so keen,

It finds its food, though it's unseen!

It listens close and takes a leap,

To catch a meal beneath the deep!

It's Time to Learn about
Arctic Fox

It eats some birds, it eats some mice,

It even steals from big wolves twice!

And when the winter makes food rare,

It follows bears to sniff and share.

The Arctic fox can run so fast,

Across the snow, it will not last.

Its paws grip ice, they do not slide,

So through the frost, it leaps with pride.

In the spring, when days grow long,

The Arctic fox sings a brand-new song.

It finds a mate and digs a den,

A home to raise its little ten!

The baby foxes, small and new,

Have coats of gray, not white or blue!

They play and learn, they run and grow,

It's Time to Learn about
Arctic Fox

Until they're strong to face the snow.

Though life is tough, they stay so smart,

With clever minds and patient hearts.

The Arctic fox survives each year,

Through cold and wind, it shows no fear.

So if you see a fox one day,

With fur so white or brown and gray,

Remember how it lives up high,

It's Time to Learn about
Arctic Fox

Beneath the stars, beneath the sky!

ABOUT THE CREATOR

Walter the Educator is one of the pseudonyms for Walter Anderson. Formally educated in Chemistry, Business, and Education, he is an educator, an author, a diverse entrepreneur, and he is the son of a disabled war veteran. "Walter the Educator" shares his time between educating and creating. He holds interests and owns several creative projects that entertain, enlighten, enhance, and educate, hoping to inspire and motivate you. Follow, find new works, and stay up to date with Walter the Educator™

at WaltertheEducator.com

www.ingramcontent.com/pod-product-compliance
Lightning Source LLC
LaVergne TN
LVHW052017060526
838201LV00059B/4068